The Critical (of self) vs. The Criticizer (of others)
How to Heal Your Depressed Brain

Stephanie Bowen, LCSW-C

www.gettingwholewithbalance.com

Contents

Preface

Too many of us find ourselves on that same unsuccessful pursuit of happiness which always seems to end at a destination of disappointment. Frustration quickly sets in after we realize our efforts have yielded nothing more than a temporary distraction. While we had high hopes for the time we spent in that meditation class or suffering through that painful caffeine cleanse, those attempts only brought a nice feeling for a short period of time. Often it feels like no matter our efforts, we cannot rid ourselves of the constant conflict occurring inside of our own brains.

There is good news though - relief from your brain is possible! There is also some bad news - your brain will continue to get in its way of happiness if the approach you have tried in the past is not adjusted.

My work as a psychotherapist has allowed me the opportunity to work alongside many people who had not yet learned this different approach. While well intended in their efforts, they found themselves stuck in a cycle generating the same undesired results. Through our work together we are able to establish a new approach to their thinking that they can then take and integrate into their lives outside of the therapy office.

In an effort to assist you, I thought it handy to assemble in one short workbook the core lessons and exercises that I introduce in psychotherapy sessions. With this information you can begin to adjust your focus and generate the results you have been wanting.

Before we dive into *how*, let's get some clarity on *why* your brain keeps getting in its own way...

Introduction

Have you ever wondered the cause of your chronic unhappiness and low self-worth? My simple answer to that complicated question: you receive persistent criticism. To expand slightly on that overly simplified answer, you have been accepting years of criticism and have been unaware that the way you are choosing to respond to your criticism is the actual cause of your unhappiness. Being unaware of your incorrect response has caused you to believe that there is a problem with *you,* and that you must accept all criticism as the truth.

Now there is one very important distinction to make here… while many people experience criticism from others, there are so many of us whose criticizer is actually ourselves. We have become our own worst critic - leading to our destroyed self-worth.

This workbook describes two very common ways people hinder themselves when they have not adjusted their response to their criticism. Learning these ways will assist you in better understanding exactly how to respond to your criticism so that it no longer hinders you. While you may not fit in one of these two profiles perfectly, you may resonate with some of the thinking patterns of one, or even both.

This short workbook will not rid you of criticism completely, but it will assist you in better reacting to it…

Chapter One
Who is a Critical (of self)?

A Critical (of self) is that person who is constantly putting their needs and their desires aside in order to accommodate the needs and desires of others. They are often consumed with sadness, frustration, and fear. Their unending pursuit of approval from everyone else has led them to a mindset of inadequacy. Sadly, Criticals have lost sight of their self-worth and are unaware that it is actually their own brain destroying their sense of self.

A Critical's well-established thinking pattern of dismissing and minimizing themselves has resulting in their inability to trust that they can make the correct decisions for themselves. They often believe that everything they do is wrong. Days are spent replaying all of the dumb things they may have ever said. Criticals spend their days comparing themselves to people who they perceive to be smarter or more successful than them.

When a Critical is invited to a party, they automatically feel a sense of intense worry or dread. They get consumed with thoughts of how to safely navigate the room without looking like a misfit. They get so good at convincing themselves that the other guests do not want them to be there. Criticals tell themselves that they are incapable of carrying on a funny or intelligent conversation. While others may be enjoying themselves, a Critical spends most of the time in their head convinced that others know that they are not good enough.

Criticals focus completely on the opinions of others when determining their own self-worth. They immediately feel sad and terrified after one perceived slight from someone else. They become consumed with fear that everyone else feels that same way and then define their entirety from one negative encounter. This cycle of thinking always leads a Critical to one place… unhappiness.

If we were to ask a Critical to list a few compliments about themselves right now, they would find themselves very flustered. Criticals can struggle with identifying even one kind thing to say about themselves at times. They actually feel like they are doing something wrong if they say something kind about themselves.

Even if a Critical can afford to pay someone to follow them around every day telling them compliment after compliment, it will not be enough. All of the compliments in the world will never be enough until the Critical actually believes themselves to be worthy of them.

A Critical may visit a physician in hopes of a medication to resolve them of their stress and exhaustion. While medicine can improve the symptoms some, it cannot resolve a Critical of their issues entirely. Today's science is just not advanced enough to fully rid a Critical of the way they are choosing to accept their criticism.

For anyone with feelings that resonates with the description above, do not worry any more than you already were before reading this. Instead, find positive in the fact that we have a better approach to your criticism! This new approach can change your focus which will in turn improve your thinking. It will be your improved thinking that will lead to your sustained happiness.

Chapter Two
Who is a Criticizer (of others)?

A Criticizer (of others) is that person in your life who has trained you to put aside your feelings in order to accommodate theirs so that you can avoid their anger. And by trained, I mean they have coerced you with your own emotional shame and guilt. If you trigger a Criticizer's anger you will be made to believe that there is something wrong with you. These people have you carefully picking and choosing your words. When you attempt to have a mature conversation with your Criticizer about how you are feeling, the topic turns to how your feelings affect them.

If you share a home or an office with a Criticizer, you can feel completely alone. Their anger and defensiveness has you avoiding communication with them. They have no regret when telling you that they will not consider your feelings until you start doing a better job of making theirs your top priority. Your efforts to have a constructive conversation prove purposeless leading you to wonder if you will ever achieve their validation of you.

Even if a Criticizer convinces you that you are nothing without them, the truth is that they are dependent on you for their emotional survival. Deep down inside, the Criticizer suffers with insecurities that lead them to believe that they are nothing without your time and attention directed at them. They have unaddressed feelings of inadequacy and believe that your desperation for their approval will make those feelings go away.

Instead of sharing these insecurities, due to a tremendous fear of being perceived as weak, they shut you down with anger. Criticizers are masterful at handing you their internal fear of not being enough and forcing you to handle it. The problem is that they hand it to you covered in criticism.

Criticizers create an inflated sense of entitlement so that they do not have to face the truth. As a result of not having developed emotional maturity, they struggle with an enormous fear that someone might point out their imperfections. This resistance makes them emotionally fragile and defensive. Rarely does a Criticizer accept responsibility for their poor behavior. Instead, they project their fears of inadequacy onto you. If you attempt to point out the truth, be prepared to feel like you are entering a war zone. You will be going up against their armor of denial and silent treatments as their weapon of choice.

Everyone gets the pleasure of dealing with a Criticizer at some point in their lives. Some can be very subtle in their efforts making it hard to detect their self-serving motives until it is too late. Unfortunately, a Criticizer can be anywhere in today's world. One may be your boss at work or your neighbor next door. They could even be your spouse, best friend, or even your grandparent.

There is very little happiness in sight for Criticizers who remain stuck in this thinking pattern. You do not have to worry about them too much though. Once someone new comes along who provides them more attention, they will leave you and you'll be left wondering what you did wrong.

If the description above describes someone close to you, do not beat up on yourself too much. The beating up on you has already occurred. Just not by you. It has instead been done by your Criticizer, who kindly directed their blows to your self-worth.

Chapter Three
Which Are You?

Chances are that if you are reading this self-help workbook you probably resonate with thinking patterns that align more with a Critical. I make this assumption because most Criticizers do not believe that they will benefit from spending their time reading something that is designed to make changes to themselves. Their desire to do introspective work is pretty minimal. Simply put, they do not self-reflect long enough to be able to acknowledge that they are actually their cause of their own interpersonal problems. Just to be sure, let's answer a few questions:

1. Do you make someone feel poorly for circumstances outside of their control?

    - Yes or No

2. Has someone ever told you that you often complain with no intention of reaching a solution?

    - Yes or No

3.   Do you end up being right nearly all of the time?

   - Yes or No

4.   Are you unable to find value in others?

   - Yes or No

5.   Do you get angry when others fail to acknowledge your accomplishments?

   - Yes or No

6.   Are you constantly worrying about upsetting someone even when you are doing something that makes you happy?

   - Yes or No

7.   Do you second guess yourself and struggle to make a decision on your own?

   - Yes or No

8.   Do you often find yourself saying 'yes' when you would rather say 'no'?

   - Yes or No

9.   Do you beat up on yourself if you make a mistake?

   - Yes or No

10. Do you spend time worrying about things outside of

your control?

- Yes or No

If you answered yes to questions 1 through 5 and no to 6

through 10, you may fall somewhere on the scale of a Criticizer.

If you answered yes to questions 6 through 10 and no to 1

through 5, you may fall somewhere on the scale of a Critical.

Criticals, your depressed brain has been tricking you into

believing that you just have to work a little harder so everyone

else will finally be satisfied with your efforts and decide you

worthy of their love and acceptance. Criticizers, your depressed

brain has been tricking you into believing that you should not

have to put in anymore effort, you are being wronged because no

one truly appreciates all that you do, and it is everyone else that

needs to change. The problem with both of these belief systems

is that they have never resulted in the happiness that you have

been wanting.

You have never been able to achieve that sustained peace

because you were not responding to your criticism correctly.

You have been so focused on your attempts to prove your

criticism wrong that you have led yourself away from happiness.

We must begin shifting your focusing away from proving

anything to your criticism. Instead, let's begin focusing on

getting in touch with your true self and remaining focused on

that despite the criticism that may continue to come your way.

Now that you know differently, you can do it better…

Chapter Four
Both Are Going About It Wrong,
So What to Do Now?

Unfortunately, babies do not come out of their mother's womb with a manual. Your parents or caregivers were not given the luxury of knowing your exact genetic predisposition. That left them forced to figure it out on their own. We can assume that if most parents had known that you would struggle with showing kindness to yourself, then they would have gone to great lengths to assist you in understanding *how* to speak compassionately to yourself. For anyone that did not receive that assistance, your brain was left to its own devices. It did exactly what it knows how to do best. It criticized.

This is where the work now begins. We must undo the negative and unkind thinking pattern that is so strongly embedded inside of your brain. Criticals must work to undo their automatic reflex to make themselves wrong and sad anytime something goes wrong. Criticizers must work to undo their automatic reflex to get angry and make someone else wrong.

Changing that well-established thinking pattern may seem impossible. This is a result of your Critical Self dominating your thoughts for so long that it has you believing it is the only way. However, that belief is untrue. The work to create new thinking patterns can be done and you will succeed at establishing them!

I imagine that your depressed brain is trying to convince you right now how unfair it is that you have work to do while others are getting off easy with their happy brains. That is untrue. No one is lucky enough to slip by without getting their assigned work to do in their lifetime. The work is different for everyone though. It is important to not compare your work to others. Some could be assigned the work of overcoming a depressed brain while others might have to battle a blood disease. What matters the most is that you agree that your approach has not been effective and you need to adjust your thinking pattern.

Now that we have identified the problem, let's get specific about the solution. Here is what you need to do now: Criticals, you must learn to turn your focus from others onto yourself. Criticizers, you must learn to turn your focus from others onto yourself. Yup! You did read that correctly. The work is the same for both. Whichever you might be, begin to focus on what you can control - yourself.

Chapter Five
The *How* So You Can Do It Better

Life is filled with challenges, but when we keep demanding that only good should be allowed to come our way we will continue to be angry, disappointed, and afraid. We must understand that life's nature is to challenge us. It is from the triumph over the challenges where we grow and learn to love ourselves deeper. Begin viewing life's challenges as lessons, not punishments.

Now that we understand that we are not being punished, we can stop resisting life. Develop a habit of approaching any challenge through exploring (not assuming) and responding (not reacting). After proper exploration, you can effectively respond.

Learning how to slow down so that you can ask yourself the useful questions when any challenge comes your way will be very important. Use the questions listed below as examples of appropriate questions that you can ask yourself during the initial exploration of a challenge:

1.   What responsibility do I hold in this situation?

2. Am I being expected to accept responsibility for things that I am not actually responsible for?

3. Am I trying to put my responsibility on someone else?

4. What are the factors in this situation that I do have control over?

5. What are the factors outside of my control?

Now that we have established the fundamentals: exploring (not assuming) and responding (not reacting), we can now add essential exercises in your journey towards happiness. Utilize the five concepts outlined below as your direct guide towards sustained peace inside your brain…

<u>5 Core Concepts:</u>

1. **Take The Second Step**

2. **You Must Get Balanced, Both Externally & Internally**
    a. **External Self**
    b. **Internal Self**

3. **Don't Make It Personal**

4. **Your Earthbound Brain Will Keep You Stuck**

5. **The 3 Golden Rules of the Balanced Self**

<u>*# 1 - Take The Second Step:*</u>

It is time to add a Second Step in your current thinking pattern. First Step thinking is easy and it is what you have been doing for most of your life. It is when you accept negative judgments and criticisms as the final truth. First Step thinking is only allowing for input from your Critical Self; however, the Critical Self is not always correct. It is designed to identify failures and make you believe you are not enough. This type of thinking will always leave you feeling wrong and depleted if not countered with input from your Confident Self.

The Second Step is the harder step but it is where you will gain peace inside your brain. This step forces you to shift your thinking from insults to compliments and your focus from pessimism to optimism. The Second Step becomes aware of the negative input from your Critical Self and it takes the time to counter it with the input from your Confident Self.

Begin making it a point to become aware of the negative comments you are saying about yourself each day. Recognize how often you routinely minimize yourself when speaking to others. Becoming aware of this habit is the first and most critical step towards change.

Your current statements about yourself might sound something like:

- × That worked out well only because I got lucky.

- × I am not sure why anyone would choose to stay with me since I do not offer anything to a relationship.

- × Things will never get better, so why try?

- × I always find a way to mess things up.

- × No one will like me if they learn who I really am.

- × I am a terrible parent if I do not participate in every one of my children's activities.

I will bet that you are excellent at telling everyone else a kind word during a time of need. You must begin turning that kindness and compassion inward as well. Allow yourself to listen to the input from your Confident Self. It is okay to think and (oh my goodness I am going to say it…) say out loud a nice thing about yourself. Challenge yourself to speak the compassionate words said by your Confident Self. Words of kindness and compassion will be the way to your sustained happiness.

The more you familiarize yourself with these Second Step statement examples below, the better you will be prepared to face the battle going on inside of your depressed brain. You must challenge that loop of negative self-talk. For too long it has been on repeat. Force yourself to challenge every unkind word you say about yourself. Re-word it to something kind and constructive like:

- ✕ ~~First Step Statement: That worked out well only because I got lucky.~~
- ✓ **Second Step Statement: I worked hard and my hard work paid off.**

- ✕ ~~First Step Statement: I am not sure why anyone would choose to stay with me since I do not offer anything to a relationship.~~
- ✓ **Second Step Statement: This relationship is not perfect, but we work at it every day.**

- ✕ ~~First Step Statement: Things will never get better, so why try?~~
- ✓ **Second Step Statement: Change is scary and I love a good challenge.**

- ✗ ~~First Step Statement: I always find a way to mess things up.~~

- ✓ **Second Step Statement: I make mistakes because I am human. I learn from those mistakes and I always do better the next time.**

  ▪

- ✗ ~~First Step Statement: No one will like me if they learn who I really am.~~

- ✓ **Second Step Statement: My imperfections are what make me strong and relatable.**

  ▪

- ✗ ~~First Step Statement: I am a terrible parent if I do not participate in every one of my children's activities.~~

- ✓ **Second Step Statement: Committing to everyone who asks for my time is not possible. I can offer my help whenever I have free time, but I also understand that my plate can only hold so much.**

Please be patient when measuring this change. It does take time. This work will not occur overnight. The pattern of using the First Step statements against yourself has been occurring for most of your life. With time and practice, the kind words of your Confident Self will come up in your conscious thinking more and more. The negative statements about yourself from your Critical Self will become less and less. Also remind yourself if you are struggling to do this work in the initial days that the

Second Step work is not the easier way, but it will be the happier

way.

<u>**# 2 - *You Must Get Balanced, Both Externally & Internally:***</u>

Time after time we all have been told that happiness comes from within. We have also heard that we must stay balanced to be healthy and happy. So we know *what* it is that we have to do, but oftentimes we struggle with *how*. In order to answer the how, let's assess your External Self and Internal Self.

a. External Self:

While it is true that happiness comes from within, we must be sure that the activities that fill our days contribute to our internal self-worth instead of detracting from it. Let's take an inventory on the activities in your life at this time. Take a minute to fill in the empty pie chart below with eight activities that consume your day-to-day and week-to-week. Some examples of these things might include work, school, family, friends, exercising, reading, gardening, etc. These activities need to be things that add consistent value to your life. Any activity like excessive drinking, drugs, gambling, shopping, etc. will not count here so do not include them in your pie slices. Those things only allow more opportunity for your Critical Self to criticize you. Fill in your pie now with your healthy eight…

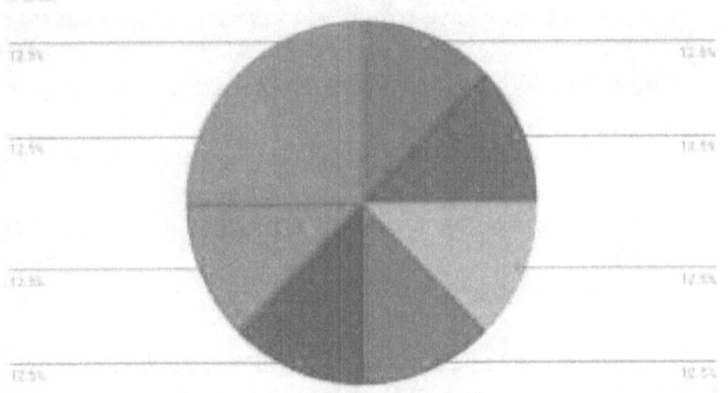

List of Your External Self Activities:

1.

2.

3.

4.

5.

6.

7.

8.

How many were you able to come up with? If you are like most, you may have struggled to identify more than four or five activities. While your depressed brain might be trying to convince you that eight is too many to manage, it is not the truth. Any number below eight will not suffice when achieving sustained happiness. It will instead lead to burnout and unhappiness. You must ensure that you have your eight and make it a point to have them on your weekly calendar. This will be a critical step in achieving a balanced brain, and the balanced brain is a happy brain.

If you are struggling to identify eight, take a minute to think back to earlier times in your life. Were there activities you used to do that brought you joy? Life may have gotten you away from doing some of your heart's hobbies. Think about those things that have fallen by the wayside. There might also be activities that you always told yourself you were not good enough to try, but you always dreamed you would someday get the chance. Well consider today that chance! Push yourself to take the Second Step even if your depressed brain tries to talk you out of activities that bring happiness in your heart.

It is important to always maintain your healthy eight at all times. These are things you do on a weekly basis. If you lose one of your eight (i.e. you get laid off from your job, your marriage ends, or are unable to access your gym or yoga studio), you must replace it with a new activity. Some examples might be: wood working, watching documentaries, cooking/baking, gardening, volunteering at your local food drive, or walking/training your dog.

If eight are not identified and given their appropriate amount of time and attention, the other activities begin to intrude on those empty slices. Failing to do this important work will make your pie quickly begin looking something like this:

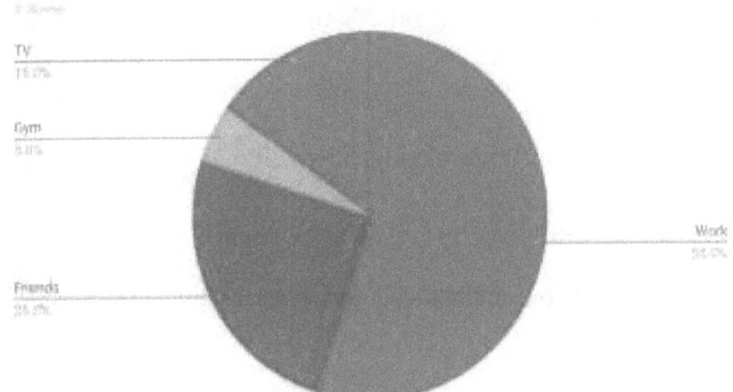

While your depressed brain may have done a good job at deceiving yourself into believing that the example above is appropriate and necessary, it is not the truth. You must learn that every slice of your pie is a priority. Believe me, your job or even your grown children will survive with only ⅛ of your pie. If you do not begin to prioritize yourself, you will be unable to give yourself the respect you require. You will continue feeling unsatisfied, which will leave you unhappy and stuck having to constantly listen to your depressed brain.

An unbalanced pie can often result from spending our time focusing on filling someone else's pie. Do not disrespect your pie anymore. You will not find happiness filling someone else's pie. People who find themselves always feeling needy and insecure are expecting more than their *one* slice of another's pie. You only get ⅛ of another's time and they only get ⅛ of yours. Stop now if you are giving more or trying to take more than *one* slice of pie. Your relationships will quickly become unhealthy if you expect more. We do not want you to be that person who gets mad for your unbalanced and unreasonable expectations.

Refer to the example below if you are struggling to create your balanced External Self pie. The activities you put in will be different, but the percentiles need to be the same. And remember, don't make any excuses for not identifying your eight…excuses keep you stuck and staying stuck keeps you sad.

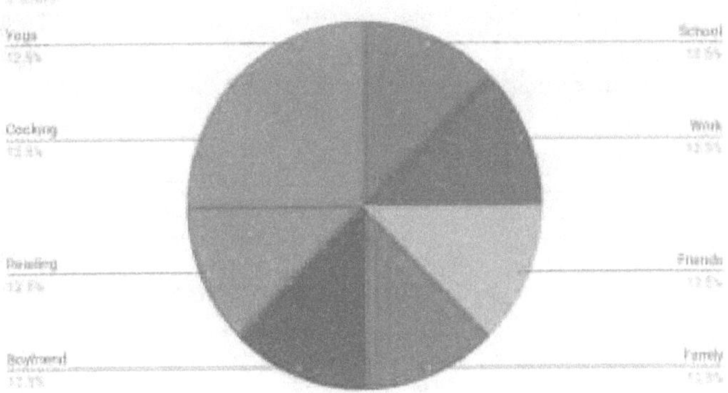

b. Internal Self:

Using that same pie, let's now take an inventory on your Internal Self. When assessing internal balance I focus on eight core traits that we find in mostly everyone. If any of the eight do not apply to you at this stage in your life, feel free to take those out and replace them with a trait that better describes you.

The eight I find most helpful when assessing for balance are:

1. <u>Introverted Self</u> – this is the part of us that requires time alone to recharge our batteries. Our time alone may be spent doing things like reading a good book, going on a run, or organizing the closets in your home.

2. <u>Extrovert Self</u> – this is the part of us that requires time with those that we love and learn from. Our time with others may be spent doing things like going to a holiday gathering, participating in a (virtual) book club with friends, or taking a jog with a neighbor.

3. <u>Confident Self</u> – this is the part of us that acknowledges our successes and encourages us to keep going when we get knocked down. This part of us tells ourselves things like, "You are stronger than your struggles," or "That scar on your chin makes you so beautifully unique."

4. <u>Critical Self</u> – this is the part of us that points out things that we need to learn from so we can do better the next time. If not properly controlled, this part of us can quickly begin defining ourselves from our mistakes and convince ourselves that we

should not receive forgiveness for them. This part of us tells ourselves things like, "You are not fast enough," or "You are not as smart as others."

5. <u>Responsible Self</u> – this is the part of us that ensures that we meet our deadlines, pays each bill, and shows up to our commitments.

6. <u>Irresponsible Self</u> – this is the part of us that allows ourselves to play hooky from work that one time, eat an extra serving of that delicious dessert, or pushes the snooze button on the alarm clock instead of getting up for that morning run.

7. <u>Creative/Artistic Self</u> – this is the part of us that enjoys the beauty in our world through things like painting, gardening, writing, music, and dance. There is a creator/artist that exists in each of us and comes through in the career path we choose and extracurricular hobbies we participate in.

8. <u>Physical/Athletic Self</u> – this is the part of us that is physically active and utilizes our muscular capabilities. This part of us is fulfilled through playing sports and exercising.

Let's get an idea of your internal balance. How often do you utilize these eight core traits throughout your days? Next to each trait below, identify the percentage that you would say you have

been giving to the trait:

Identify the percentile next to each trait:

1. Introverted Self: ______

2. Extrovert Self: ______

3. Confident Self:______

4. Critical Self: ______

5. Responsible Self: ______

6. Irresponsible Self: ______

7. Creative/Artistic Self: ______

8. Physical/Athletic Self: ______

Total: <u>100%</u>

Each person comes pre-wired with those core internal traits at birth. It is our responsibility to ensure that we honor each by giving it its appropriate amount of time and attention. It is also our responsibility to not allow one trait to dominate or intrude on another trait's time. The goal is to give each internal trait its ⅛.

Below is an example of a balanced Internal Self. This is a person who makes themselves a top priority:

Balanced Internal Self:

1. Introverted Self: 12.5%

2. Extrovert Self: 12.5%

3. Confident Self: 12.5%

4. Critical Self: 12.5%

5. Responsible Self: 12.5%

6. Irresponsible Self: 12.5%

7. Creative/Artistic Self: 12.5%

8. Physical/Athletic Self: 12.5%

Total: 100%

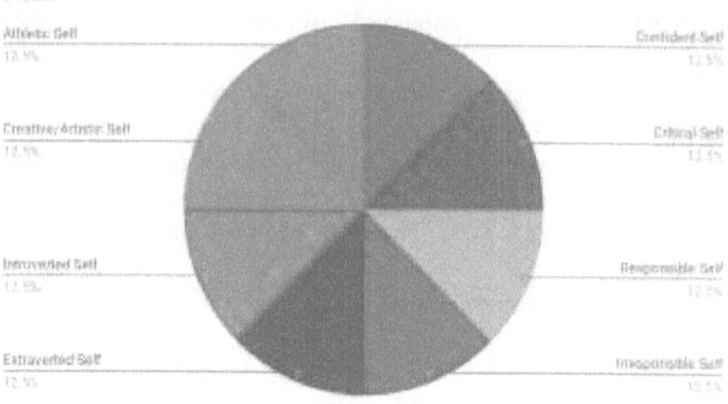

What occurs too often inside a depressed brain is that the Critical Self, Responsible Self, and Introvert Self begin to dismiss the input of the other five traits. The constant repetition of insults and minimizing of one's self without any encouragement or positivity from the other traits begins to mute the Confident Self, Extrovert Self, Irresponsible Self, Creative/Artistic Self, and Active/Athletic Self.

If you are killing yourself with overtime at work, telling yourself that you are a horrible employee for wanting to take a vacation, or avoiding social activities because they only bring you more mental exhaustion, your pie is unbalanced. This imbalance will manifest in all different ways, but they always lead to more unhappiness.

Too often your depressed brain tries to convince you that there is no way to get off that career path you hate, you must overwork yourself to get to some stability, or you have to remain in a relationship with someone who leaves you emotionally drained. A depressed brain left to its own devices will begin looking something like this:

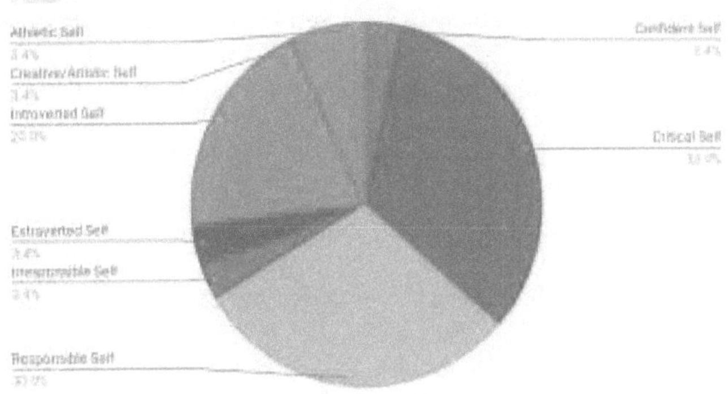

If you are stuck in a pattern of giving, giving, giving, you will leave nothing left for yourself. This leads to exhaustion and frustration. Day after day you will come home exhausted from a long day of giving, pass out early, wake up still feeling exhausted, and then repeat the same pattern all over again the following day. You must begin giving yourself approval to use some of your own energy on yourself. Tell yourself that you are not wrong for taking time to do your Second Step work. Believe you are worth it!

I understand that our Critical Self can too quickly begin convincing ourselves that we are not worth it; however, you must know that it is not true. While it is easy to understand why someone would feel this way if they have only been listening to the input from their Critical Self their entire lives, it is a disservice to ourselves when we only allow input from ⅛ of ourselves to be heard. Just because the Critical Self is the loudest, does not mean it is always correct.

Taking the time to do your Second Step work will allow you to get back in touch with your other internal traits. I bet you have been missing those traits too! Allow for the input from your Confident Self, Irresponsible Self, Physical/Active Self, Creative/Artistic Self, and Extraverted Self to be heard. Validate their input without allowing your Critical Self and Responsible

Self to immediately shut them down. Honoring all of your traits will bring your balance.

Before your brain gets too busy convincing you that you do not have time to do this work, let's quickly dive in…Begin by reminding yourself of all of your wonderful attributes. In the space below, write down five compliments about yourself. Please spend around thirty seconds on this. Be sure that your compliments are not things like, "I am the person that everyone goes to at work when something has to get done," or "I am really good at cleaning up my children's messes." Those are not the type of compliments I am talking about here. Cleaning up their own mess is something your children might actually be able to do themselves, and overcompensating at work so that you feel worthy is only reinforcing your Critical Self.

Write your list of five kind things about yourselves below:

1.

2.

3.

4.

5.

Was it challenging to list five in thirty seconds? Too often we all struggle in this area and can get stuck after only listing two or three. If you did struggle it is an indicator that your Critical Self is dominating your thinking. It has also done a good job of convincing you that it is wrong or conceited to praise yourself. As a result, you have withheld vital kind self-talk that you need to hear from yourself.

We all can think back and too quickly recall perceived insults someone has said to us; however, we too quickly dismiss or ignore the compliments that have come. Insults are powerful and they add up quickly if the Critical Self remains in control of our thinking. We must shift our focus from our Critical Self to our Confident Self in order to improve our thinking.

Researchers have actually studied the power of positive comments to negative comments within business teams and marriages. Marcial Losada and Emily Heaphy (2004) determined in their research study that the number of positive comments to the number of negative comments was the factor that made the greatest difference in determining the business team's success or failure. They determined that the highest-performing teams used nearly six positive comments to every one negative comment.

John Mordechai Gottman's research for his book <u>What Predicts Divorce? The Relationship Between Marital Processes and Marital Outcomes</u> (1993) found that the largest determinant of a marriage's success or failure was the ratio of positive comments to negative comments. He determined the optimal ratio in a healthy marriage had five positive comments to every one negative comment.

Since we understand that the human brain is highly sensitive to insults and can easily dwell in the negative, taking the Second Step here is crucial. You must work to ensure that the number of unkind words you say to yourself does not outnumber the amount of kind words. I recommend that you utilize the researcher's one to five (1:5) ratio when speaking to yourself. That means every time you insult yourself, you immediately tell yourself five compliments. If you count ten negative comments over the course of one day, you then have FIFTY compliments to begin listing about yourself. If you struggled to list five compliments in the exercise above, you really have your work cut out for you.

There is a very easy way to get out of having to keep up with this 1:5 ratio... do not criticize yourself. However, since we know that you are new to this and the likelihood of immediately discontinuing a behavior that you have been doing for many years is slim, be sure to have your long list on hand.

<u>**# 3 – *Don't Make It Personal:***</u>

Has someone ever walked past you without saying 'hello' and you instantly began replaying in your head all of your interactions to identify what you did wrong? Take the Second Step so that you no longer make everything about you. Our Critical Self tries to convince us that everything is a result of our mistakes, even when it has nothing to do with us. Consider the possibility that that person who did not acknowledge you was deep in thought or having a really difficult day. Odds are that it was not related to anything you did at all.

If for some reason they did intentionally ignore you, then that is immature. I would recommend that you find the positive in no longer having to be friendly with someone who withholds verbal communication from you. If they were really ignoring you, there is an internal imbalance within them that requires further investigation on their end...not yours.

It is very important that you no longer take on other's internal issues. When we take on other people's issues we are actually searching for a way to quiet our Critical Self through receiving external validation. We incorrectly believe that the praise of others will quiet our Critical Self, but it does not work that way. The only way to quiet our Critical Self is to do it from inside of ourselves. It is only through validating the input of our other internal traits that we can quiet the criticism and balance out our Critical Self.

Another problem with using others to solve our internal imbalance is that we keep others from doing their own Second Step work. If you delay them in doing their work, they will remain unbalanced. The unbalanced Internal Self leads to more insecurity and dissatisfaction and the chaos between you will ensue.

Now that you know this new way you can stop setting yourself up for failure. Let's save you from anymore unnecessary stress or wasting of your precious time. Focus on taking the Second Step and allowing other's to do their Second Step work. That is what will lead to peace and balance sooner than later, for everyone.

Fear is not held in the heart. It is only found in our earthbound brain. We must learn to put more value in our hearts if we want sustained peace. Doing your Second Step work will allow you to better distinguish between your heart's desires and your earthbound brain's self-imposed fear.

If there is someone in your life that makes you feel wrong for what is in your heart, ask yourself if there is something that they actually fear? Is it possible that their unspoken fear and unhappiness is just being disguised? Following advice from an unbalanced brain will lead to failure for both of you.

Do not let yourself be held back by someone else's fear and unhappiness. Encourage them to speak their concerns, but do not allow them to make you wrong about the things that are right in your heart.

It is very important to accept only the input of others who are externally and internally balanced. You will know that they are balanced through their solution-focused approach. Balanced people do not insult; they will provide constructive feedback when asked. They will encourage you to face your fears and suggest new ways to work around them. A balanced brain always looks to learn from mistakes so that they can do better in the future.

If your earthbound brain has already started listing off all of the reasons why your heart is wrong, minimize that fear by instead making a list of your heart's goals. These goals have gone ignored for too long. Make an action plan so that you can begin working towards your heart's goals. Trust that you will achieve them.

Learn to stand up to your earthbound brain. Don't be responsible for keeping yourself stuck. Staying stuck keeps you frustrated and depressed. Gently push through your fears by taking one small step at a time. It is healthy to take risks at times and always remember to trust your heart. It will be lead you to amazing places!

Follow these three rules as much as you possibly can. They will strengthen your heart and help you release the fear inside of your earthbound brain:

1. **Focus On The Things You Can Control -** You can only control yourself. Remind yourself of this every day, all day. It does not serve you to focus only on identifying the things other people need to change. Instead, ask yourself how you can change your approach to them? Create a new pattern of confronting criticism with questions.

2. **Allow Others to Do Their Work -** You cannot control, fix, or change anyone but yourself. If someone has not given you consent to assist them, the only thing you can do for them is to love them. You may even have to love them from afar at times. When they do ask for your assistance, then you can help. Learn to let them do their Second Step work so that they can achieve peace sooner.

3. **You Choose Your Words, So Make Them Kind** - Make it a point to speak kindly in all conversations with yourself and with others. Approach every problem with a solution-focused mindset. Ask yourself what you can do to leave others better than they were prior to their interaction with you. Stay away from accusations, judgments, and criticizing as often as possible. Those things can keep you held you back from achieving sustained happiness.

Conclusion
Let's Not Call This The End
Because It's Just the Beginning for You

Achieving peace is possible! Begin by deciding right now that you are no longer going to define yourself by the input of your Critical Self. Accept and validate the input from your other internal traits as well. Use the 5 Core Concepts as a starting point on this new journey.

Results will not occur overnight. We are working to disrupt thinking patterns that were established many years ago. Be patient with yourself during this process. It takes time to make large changes.

Ask for help when you need it. Turn to your therapist. We can assist you when you become stuck. It is important that you remind yourself that everyone becomes stuck at some points in life. Do not let your Critical Self convince you that you are the only one because that is simply untrue.

View your work in therapy like a new course that you have agreed to take and your therapist like that of an advisor. This course will be very different than any course you took in school though. It will be focused completely on your approach to yourself. The purpose will be to teach you how to better respect and love *you*.

Be prepared for your therapist to share with you their recommendations on your life. Hear those recommendations out. We want to assist you in approaching things from another angle. Hopefully we can offer a new angle you have not yet tried and assist you in feeling better prepared to handle your life's challenges. What is most important is that you use your therapist to assist you in perfecting your Second Step work.

Begin today to ask yourself how you can change your focus, thinking, and approach. Take responsibility for the things that are within your control while learning to no longer punish yourself for things outside of your control. Do not place the blame on others if you are in fact responsible. Implement personal boundaries with those that insist that you take responsibility for their internal issues. And always remember to stay focused on your end goal...to heal your depressed brain. Good luck!

References

John Mordechai Gottman (1993). *What Predicts Divorce? The Relationship Between Marital Processes and Marital Outcomes.* Psychology Press; 1 edition (November 1, 1993)

M. Losada and E. Heaphy (2004). The Role of Positivity and Connectivity in the Performance of Business Teams: A Nonlinear Dynamics Model. American Behavioral Scientist, vol. 47, 6: pp. 740-765.